A FESTIVAL FOR FROGS

Funny Poems for Kids

Kenn Nesbitt

Illustrations by
Rafael Domingos

Published by
Purple Room Publishing
1037 NE 65th St #81845
Seattle, WA 98115

Fax: 800-991-2996
ATTN: Purple Room Publishing #81845

www.poetry4kids.com

For Jack

Contents

A Festival for Frogs

We're at the Frog Fiesta.
It's a festival for frogs,
where the frogs are dancing happily
in cowboy boots and clogs.

They parade in wide sombreros
and in brightly colored shirts,
or they swing and sway in circles
in their broad embroidered skirts.

They are bopping to the melodies
of famous froggy songs,
or they're croaking to the choruses
of froggy sing-alongs.

It's a hopping hootenanny
on a lovely summer's eve.
It's a dance that's so fantastic.
It's a bash you can't believe.

And it's on a night like this one,
near a bayou, on a bog,
that I sometimes make a little wish...
I wish to be a frog.

My Kitten Is a Ninja

My kitten is a ninja.
He wears a black disguise.
He sneaks up on me stealthily
and takes me by surprise.

I never hear him coming.
He doesn't make a peep.
He hides, then glides in silently
and makes a flying leap.

I don't know why he does it.
The reason isn't clear.
He simply likes to tackle me
then swiftly disappear.

I wish that he was normal
and didn't act like that.
My life would be so different if
I had an average cat.

I'd play with him, and pet him,
and treat him gingerly.
Instead, whenever he's around
I get a ninjury.

Benjamin Blink Drank Invisible Ink

Benjamin Blink
drank invisible ink.
It wasn't a smart thing to do.
He gulped a glass down,
gave a burp, then a frown,
and instantly vanished from view.

His parents went wild
and they cried, "Where's our child?
We saw him a minute ago.
It's honestly weird
that our boy disappeared.
Oh, where did our Benjamin go?

"He's faded away
and we can't really say
the nature of Benjamin's plight."
But Ben hadn't died
so, he promptly replied,
"I'm here, but I'm clear out of sight."

He said, "Mom and Dad,
I can see this looks bad
but surely, there must be a way
our family physician
can fix my condition.
Let's go to the doctor today.

They drove little Ben
to the hospital then
and explained what had happened, and how.
The nurse shook her head
at poor Ben as she said,
"The doctor can't see you right now."

So, Ben is still there,
though it may seem unfair,
and the nurse might appear to be mean,
but Benjamin Blink
drank invisible ink
and now has to wait to be seen.

The Man from Planet X

His name is Rex from Planet X,
the man from outer space.
He loves to visit other worlds
and flies from place to place.

He always eats on Planet 8
and drinks on Planet T.
He'll often golf on Planet 4
and sail on Planet C.

You'll sometimes find him visiting
the Planet U-R-2,
or playing hide-and-seek with friends
on Planet I-C-U.

He always plays the lottery
on Planet O-I-1.
And goes to planet I-M-B-4-U-R
just for fun.

His favorite place to sleep is
Planet Z-Z-Z-Z.
It's best if you don't ask me
what he does on Planet P.

Unsteady Teddy

I have a little teddy bear
I like to hug and hold.
But yesterday I told my mom,
"I think he has a cold."

I said, "I heard him sniffle,
and he seems to have a chill.
His forehead feels a little hot.
I swear my bear is ill.

"Let's take him to the doctor
who can diagnose diseases,
and cure him of his sniffles
and his shivers and his sneezes."

My mother said, "Don't worry dear.
You might not be aware,
but sniffles aren't uncommon
in your average teddy bear."

She said, "His nose is runny
and his eyes are red and puffy.
But no, he doesn't have a cold.
He's just a little stuffy."

I Helped My Mom Make Dinner

I helped my mom make dinner.
(I like to help a lot.)
I helped make mashed potatoes
until I dropped the pot.

I helped her roast a turkey.
I helped her bake a pie.
The oven started smoking.
I really don't know why.

I helped her set the table.
I dropped the dinner rolls.
I helped arrange the dishes.
I broke a pair of bowls.

I helped her pour the milk.
I spilled it on the floor.
I helped so much she said
she didn't need help anymore.

Hank the Helpful Helper

I'm Hank the Helpful Helper.
I'm helpful as can be.
I'll help you spend your money.
I'll help you watch TV.

I'll help you read your comics
and play with all your toys.
I'll help you mess your room up
and make a lot of noise.

I'll help you pet your kitten.
I'll help you fly your drone.
I'll help you open presents
and play games on your phone.

I'll help you eat your ice cream,
your cookies, and your cakes.
I'll help you drink your sodas,
your smoothies, and your shakes.

Now, some things I can't help with
but really, just a few...
I can't help with your homework
or chores you have to do.

But if it's really easy
and super fun to do,
I'm ready to be helpful.
So, how can I help you?

As I Was Walking Down the Street

As I was walking down the street
there was a man I didn't meet
because he wasn't there to see
and so, he didn't notice me.

If he were there, I might have said,
"Your hat goes nicely with your head,"
then smiled at him and walked away,
except he wasn't there that day.

In fact, he wasn't there before
or afterward, and nevermore
shall I espy that man I missed
because that man does not exist.

That's why I never said, "Hello,"
or shook his hand or watched him go.
I'm pretty sure he didn't care
because I also wasn't there.

A Random Poem

I read a random poem.
It was full of random text.
I couldn't tell banana what
words might come pencil next.

In donut nearly every line
it had a random word.
This poem was the cat most
football random I had heard.

I wondered fish who wrote it.
Was the poet spoon insane?
What pickle sort of person
had this baseball kind of brain?

The more I doorknob read it
the more house cow it became.
It also square spaghetti frog
gorilla gumball game.

At last, it uncle soccer cheese
in over why no what
until explosive chicken helmet
uh-oh sparkle butt.

Pizza, Pizza, I Love You

Pizza,   Pizza,

I love you. And   I hope you love

me too. Crust and sauce and melty cheese

have me begging on my knees. You're

my favorite. You're so fine.

Won't you be my

Valentine

?

Bow Wow Wow, Meow Meow

Bow wow wow.　　Meow, meow.

My dog and cat are　friends somehow.

My dog says, "Woof!" My cat says, "Purr."

They hug and lick each other's fur.

I'm glad I have a dog and cat.

I love them both,

and that is

that.

My Dog Is Always Shivering

My dog is always shivering.
He always seems so cold.
And so, I got some clothes for him
where pet supplies are sold.

I bought my dog a sweater,
and some mittens, and a hat.
I even turned the heat up
on the household thermostat.

But still, my dog was chilly
so, I purchased him a pair
of insulated overalls
and thermal underwear.

I put him in a parka
and a fleecy winter vest.
I thought he would be hot.
My dog's completely overdressed.

He's now beside the fireplace
with its big old flaming log.
And yet he sits there shivering.
My dog's a chilly dog.

My New Remote

I bought a new remote control
to turn on my TV.
They said it worked with everything.
I brought it home to see.

I aimed it at my puppy.
I mean, why not take a chance?
I pushed the Power button
and my dog began to dance.

I aimed it at my parakeet
and gently pressed Rewind.
It started singing backward
which completely blew my mind.

I tried it on my father.
When I lightly clicked on Play,
he said, "Hey, why don't you and I
go kick a ball today?"

I tried it on my mother
and she brought me chocolate cake.
And that was when I might
have made a really big mistake.

I accidentally clicked on Pause
while pointing at my face.
Can someone please come click this thing?
I froze myself in place.

I Tried to Play Soccer

I tried to play soccer.
The ball hit my face.
My nose started bleeding
all over the place.

I tried to play rugby.
I slipped on the field.
I scraped up my elbows.
They still haven't healed.

I tried to play tennis.
I tripped on the net.
The bump on my head
is the biggest one yet.

I tried to play baseball.
I got a black eye.
I wasn't quite able
to catch that pop fly.

Our team always loses.
It's me the coach blames.
So, now I stay home and
play video games.

We Call Our Teacher Mister E.

We call our teacher Mister E.
His last name is a mystery.
It's secret, but we don't know why.
We think that maybe he's a spy
who doesn't share his name so he
can hide his real identity.

Now, someday that last name of his
may tell us who he really is,
but only if we get to see
the true last name of Mister E.
Until then, there will always be
the mystery of Mister E.

Our Math Teacher's Missing

Our math teacher's missing.
He cannot be found.
We've looked high and low but
he's nowhere around.

We peeked in the classrooms.
We peered through the doors.
We looked in the lockers
and dug through the drawers.

We dropped by the office.
We searched in the halls.
We ran through the bathrooms
inspecting the stalls.

He's not on the playground
or out on the lawn.
It's hard to believe but
our math teacher's gone.

We can't say for sure but
we're starting to think
it could be because we
have sort of a stink.

And probably nothing
has happened to him.
He just knows our math class
is right after gym.

I Fell in a Well

When I was hiking yesterday
I fell into a well.
I tumbled to the bottom
and let out a painful yell.
And just in case you're wondering
the reason that I fell...
I didn't have my glasses on
and couldn't see that well.

I Built a Big Building

I built a big building for building big buildings.
My building was massive and wide.
And inside that building I built a new building
for building more buildings inside.

And in that new building I built one more building.
And in there I built several more.
With every new building inside the last building,
I kept building buildings galore.

I don't know how many new buildings I built,
but it must have been dozens or scores.
Unfortunately, I'm now trapped in the last one.
I didn't build windows or doors.

Help!

Please help me! I'm stuck in this book.
I've tried but I cannot get out.
I'm jumping and waving
and ranting and raving.
Can you really not hear me shout?

I'm not even sure how it happened
I ended up under the page.
I woke up this morning
without any warning
to find myself trapped in this cage.

I've tried crawling under the bottom.
I've tried climbing over the top.
But no one will free me.
They can't even see me
no matter how high that I hop.

I've left you a voice mail message.
I've sent a few texts with my phone.
I'm knocking. I'm banging.
I'm pounding. I'm clanging.
And yet I'm still in here alone.

I hope that you'll come to my rescue.
I know that the chance is remote.
But still, it's worth trying
and better than crying,
So, that's why I wrote you this note.

Lost Inside a Labyrinth

I'm lost inside a labyrinth.
I'm stuck inside a maze.
I'm not sure how it happened but
I've been in here for days.

I should have paid attention
when I took that fateful turn
and stepped in absent-mindedly
without the least concern.

You see, what I had thought would be
an ordinary hike
is now a maze of twisty little
tunnels, all alike.

I'm looking left. I'm looking right.
I'm staring straight ahead,
but can't decide which path to take.
It's filling me with dread.

I've tried to find some kind of sign
that shows which way to go.
And now that I've run into you,
I wonder if you know?

If we just work together,
I expect we'll be okay.
So, if you have a moment,
won't you help me find the way?

My Father Was a Janitor

My father was a janitor.
My mom thought he was sweet.
She fell for him the day they met.
He swept her off her feet.

I Got My Mom a Valentine

I got my mom a Valentine,
the coolest one I've seen.
It wasn't purple, pink, or red;
my card was brownish-green.

I thought it was a perfect piece
of Valentine's Day art.
With nothing written on it,
it was just a big green heart.

I gave it to my mother.
I was sure she'd be amused.
Instead, she looked at me and said,
"I'm totally confused."

I guess it wasn't obvious.
She didn't have a clue
my brownish-greenish card was just
to tell her, "Olive hue."

The Eggs Were All Bedeviled

The eggs were all bedeviled
after having been belayed
and begotten by the chef who then
had all of them betrayed.

The tray was then beheld
until the table was beset
and the people were becoming
for the eggs they would beget.

While most became on time that day,
befriends who were belated
did not belove the eggs because
they weren't too well-berated.

They said they ate benign of them
but only ate before,
(a belittle white belie
before beheading out the door).

They stopped before believing
and bespoke belong till dawn,
then began a new bequest
for better eggs and were begone.

My Job at the Calendar Factory

I worked at the calendar factory.
I loved it in so many ways.
To color the numbers was always
the highlight of all of the days.

But one day I felt pretty lousy.
I had a bad cold and a cough.
They fired me then from the factory
for trying to take a day off.

I went to the doctor that morning.
He said, "It's a good thing you're here.
It looks like your days are now numbered.
I'd give you six months to a year.

"I wish that your life could be longer
but that's not the case, I'm afraid.
You might live till March or till April."
It's fair to say I was dismayed.

For fourteen days I was too weak.
But then I got better somehow,
and I've walked away from that factory.
Those days are behind me for now.

My Lunch Gave Me a Tummy Ache

My lunch gave me a tummy ache,
a tummy ache,
a tummy ache.
My lunch gave me a tummy ache.
I really don't know why.

I only ate a sirloin steak,
a birthday cake,
a chocolate shake.
It wasn't hard, for goodness sake.
I didn't even try.

See, lunch was at this big buffet,
with fish fillet,
and cheese soufflé.
I even tried the crème brûlée,
and liverwurst on rye.

I might have had spaghetti too,
some cheese fondue,
a bowl of stew,
then wasn't quite sure what to do.
I felt like I could cry.

But still, I ate the roasted ham,
the leg of lamb,
the candied yam,
and after that, some random jam.
I think I'm gonna die.

It feels as if I'm gonna burst.
It's just the worst.
I must be cursed.
But if I'm gonna die, then first...
I'd better try the pie.

Payton the Painter

Payton is a painter.
She's the speedy painting queen.
She paints her pictures quicker
than the world has ever seen.

She splashes paint so rapidly,
her motion is a blur.
As artists go, there's no one else
who's quite as fast as her.

She's fond of painting animals
and plants and people too.
She'll often paint a landscape
or a lovely sunset view.

She'll tell you, "This one is a cat,
and this one is a house,
and this one is a rocket ship,
and this one is a mouse."

It's hard to tell for certain, though.
They all just look like slop.
She doesn't paint them with a brush.
She paints them with a mop.

My New TV

I bought a really cheap TV.
It only cost a buck.
They said it was on sale because
the volume knob was stuck.

I took it home and turned it on.
THE SOUND WAS WAY TOO LOUD!!!
The volume knob was stuck on high.
But still, I felt so proud.

My TV was the cheapest one
in any store in town.
It only cost a dollar so
I couldn't turn it down.

While Lying on the Lawn

While lying on lawn at school
I saw a cloud float by.
It looked just like my math book
as it drifted through the sky.

Another cloud went gliding by,
erasers and some glue.
I saw my backpack amble past,
my calculator too.

I watched in wordless wonder
as the gentle breezes blew,
while clouds that looked like binders
and construction paper flew.

The school bell rang and startled me.
I woke up on the grass.
Just like a cloud, I'd drifted off.
I'd better get to class.

Last Night I Made Friends with a Giant

Last night I made friends with a giant,
an elf, and a unicorn too.
I swam with a beautiful mermaid,
then climbed on a dragon and flew.

I went to a ball in a castle.
I partied with princes and queens.
I rescued a girl from a tower.
I purchased some magical beans.

I helped a few pigs build their houses,
then ran from some bears and a witch,
uncovered a cave full of treasure,
and ended up famous and rich.

I had all these awesome adventures.
An evening was all that it took.
I'm glad that I happened to doze off
while reading a fairy-tale book.

Busy Jack

Jack went up a beanstalk,
and Jack went up a hill.
Then Jack fell down and broke his crown
along with his friend Jill.

Then Jack jumped over a candlestick.
He also built a house.
And as for fat, he can't eat that.
He gives it to his spouse.

He's known for killing giants and
he brings the winter season
with snow and frost. If he's exhausted,
now you know the reason.

So, Jack sits in the corner now
and eats his Christmas pie.
I think that Jack deserves some slack.
He's such a busy guy.

The Dragons are Dozing

The dragons are dozing.
They're catching some Z's.
They're snoozing and snoring
as loud as they please.

They snore through the morning.
They drowse through the day.
They frequently dream
the whole evening away.

And then, after sunset,
the dragons will rise.
They'll wake from their slumber
and take to the skies.

They'll search for a snack,
like a sheep or some cattle,
then fly around looking
for knights they can battle.

By morning, they're worn out
and rest while it's light.
They sleep every day since
they fight every knight.

My Purple Unicorn

I have a purple unicorn.
I keep him as a pet.
He has a single purple horn.
He's had it since we met.

He also has a purple tail.
He has a purple hide.
He's purple on the front and back
and purple on each side.

He has a purple head and neck.
He has a purple mane.
I'll bet, inside his purple skull,
he has a purple brain.

I know you think I'm joking,
that this simply can't be true.
You're right. That was a lie. In truth...
My unicorn is blue.

Michael the Psychic

I'm Michael the Psychic, superlative seer.
The future, to me, is exceedingly clear.
Predicting tomorrow is easy for me.
I study the stars and I suddenly see.

I look at my tea leaves to know of next week.
A month or two later takes just one more peek.
I enter a marvelous, mystical trance,
and learn what will happen a year in advance.

A glance at your palm will allow me to say
the things that will happen a decade away.
A roll of the dice or the turn of a card,
and even a century isn't that hard.

The winter, the summer, the spring, and the fall,
divulge all their secrets in my crystal ball.
I'm sure of tomorrow but who could have guessed
today we would have an arithmetic test?

My Brother's Insistent

My brother's insistent.
Whenever we play,
he always insists that
we do things his way.
He's good at insisting.
When we disagree,
he has to insist he
knows better than me.

He's always insisted
that he should go first,
insisted he's best and
insisted I'm worst.
He also insists that
he's right and I'm wrong,
insisting consistently
all morning long.

My brother's insistence...
it might be my bad.
They misunderstood when
I told mom and dad
I wanted some siblings,
and like a tongue twister,
they thought that I asked for
a brother insister.

My Gramma Got a Camera

My gramma got a camera
from my grampa as a gift.
She started snapping pictures.
She was speedy. She was swift.

She posted loads of photos,
sharing lots of shots online,
and got a zillion likes for her
expression and design.

She started taking selfies
and recording videos,
which gained her lots of followers
since she was good at those.

Some days she'll post a portrait
or a landscape panorama.
And now you know the reason why
I call her Instagramma.

I Need to Do My Homework

I need to do my homework now.
I really shouldn't wait.
If I don't do it right away,
my homework will be late.

But first I'll check my messages.
Oh, look, I got a text.
I probably should answer it,
then do my homework next.

My friend says there's a video
I simply have to see.
I'll watch it first,
and do my homework momentarily.

But now I'm feeling hungry so,
I guess I need a snack.
I'll get myself a bite to eat
and then I'll come right back.

Oh, hey, I just remembered
there's a game I want to play.
Just twenty minutes won't make
that much difference anyway.

I'd better do my homework now
and not procrastinate.
Except, oh no! It's time for bed...
My homework will be late.

The School Year Is Over

The school year is over.
The summer is here.
At last, it's my favorite
time of the year.

The summer's a season
no others can match.
I'll go to the park
to play Frisbee and catch.

I'll get to play daily
outside in the sun.
I'll roll on the lawn
or I'll go for a run.

I'll jump in the pool
to cool off from the heat.
Whenever I'm hungry
I'll ask for a treat.

It's all so exciting.
It's awesome. It's cool.
I'm glad I'm a dog when
my kid's home from school.

When Puppies Play Baseball

When puppies play baseball
they like to have fun.
They race and they roll
as they run in the sun.

They jump and they bump and
they tumble all day.
It's always exciting
to watch as they play.

But nobody wins and
they don't score at all.
Because, if they catch it,
they chew up the ball.

Dad in the Sand

I buried my dad at
the beach in the sand.
He asked for my help so
I gave him a hand.

He wanted a way to
stay out of the sun,
and told me he thought that
it sounded like fun.

I kind of forgot where
I buried him, though.
I hope I can find him.
Mom's ready to go.

Everyone's Screaming

Everyone's screaming and running away.
They're fleeing the beach in a panic today.
They're heading for home in a heck of a hurry.
It's something to see as they scramble and scurry.

Some run like a rabbit. Some flap like a goose.
Some jump like a monkey, or scoot like a moose.
Some leap like a lemur, or bound like a bear,
or sprint like a stallion, or maybe a mare.

Some spring like a cheetah or hop like a frog.
This started the second I called for my dog.
This never occurs when we go to the park.
I'm thinking I shouldn't have named my dog "Shark."

The Sand Looks Like Candy

The sand looks like candy.
I'm licking my lips.
The ocean is soda.
The seashells are chips.

The beachballs are berries.
The snorkels are fries.
And all the umbrellas
and frisbees are pies.

The sun is a pizza
or maybe a peach.
I seem to be hungry
today at the beach.

A Sweet Story

An alien landed outside on the lawn,
all slimy, and grimy, and green.
He showed up this morning exactly at dawn
in his alien flying machine.

He broke down our door and invaded our house,
exploring for something to eat.
He rummaged through cupboards and foraged in drawers
in search of a snack that was sweet.

He feasted on candies and jellies and jams.
He ate every cookie and cake.
He blended our ice cream with sugar and syrup,
and slurped it all down as a shake.

He gobbled our waffles and cinnamon rolls.
He guzzled our soda and juice.
He chewed up our chocolates and fed on our fudge.
He munched all our muffins and mousse.

And when he was done eating all our desserts,
he wandered back out through the door
and left us with nothing else yummy to eat.
We might need to go to the store.

How Not to Cook

To be a chef, you need to learn
techniques for cooking foods.
I have a list of those techniques
and here's what it includes...

It's perfect if you fry the fries.
It's great to toast the toast.
It's alright if you char the chard.
It's good to roast the roast.

It's fine to pickle pickles
and to smooth the smoothies too,
and stuffing stuff in stuffing
is a splendid thing to do.

It's true that you can stew the stew,
and you can shake the shakes,
and dip the dips, and whip the whips,
and maybe stake the steaks.

Why, you could even grill the grill,
and you could spice the spice,
and microwave the microwave,
and ice the ice with ice.

But one technique that isn't found
in any guide or book
is something you should never do...
Don't ever cook the cook.

Making Cakes

I use a bunch of carrots
when I make a carrot cake.
And chocolate's what I need
when chocolate cake is what I bake.

My corncake has a lot of corn.
My cheesecake calls for cheese.
My apple cake needs apples
so, I use a few of these.

And when I make banana cake
bananas fill the bill.
Some ice cream is the thing that gives
my ice cream cake its chill.

Today I'm craving something new
and so, I'm making plans
to try two brand new recipes...
I'll need some cups and pans.

I Came Upon Some Words

I came upon some words that had
been scattered on the ground
as if someone had tossed them there
in hopes that they'd be found.

I picked them up and brought them home.
I read them one by one,
then started rearranging them
in sentences for fun.

The sentences formed stanzas
on the floor throughout my home.
I know it might seem strange but
that is how I made this poem.

I took the words outside again
and scattered them around.
I tossed them out and left them there
in hopes that they'd be found.

So, if you come upon these words
I hope you bring them home
and play with them to see if you
can make another poem.

How to Write a Very Long Poem

If
you
want
to
write
a
poem
and
to
make
it
nice
and
long,
you
should
try
this
little
writing
trick.
You
really
can't
go
wrong.

It's
a
tried
and
tested
method,
or
at
least
that's
what
I've
heard,
if
you
make
sure
every
line
you
write
has
just
one
single
word.

I Let My Mind Wander

Whenever there's something
I think I should ponder,
I'll drift in a daydream
and let my mind wander.

My mind will meander
and ramble and roam,
and flitter and flutter
a long way from home.

It randomly ambles
through theory and thought.
It thinks about things
it was probably taught.

It flickers through feelings.
It dances through dreams.
It contemplates concepts
and sketches out schemes.

It likes to go rolling
and strolling astray
until it has practically
wandered away.

But now I'm confounded
and all out of whack.
Today my mind wandered
and never came back.

I Found a Penny on the Ground

I found a penny on the ground
and thought it might bring luck.
And so, I tried to pick it up
but found that it was stuck.

I pulled a little harder but
it wasn't any use.
I went and got a crowbar.
Still, I couldn't pry it loose.

I whacked it with a hammer till,
at last, I got it free,
but accidentally struck my thumb,
and tripped and skinned my knee.

A dog then chased me down the street
as it began to rain.
I almost got run over by
a taxi and a train.

I slammed into a garbage can
which covered me in crud.
And just before I made it home,
I slipped and fell in mud.

At last, I climbed in bed,
then felt a headache coming on.
I couldn't sleep at all that night.
I tossed and turned till dawn.

That penny brought me luck alright,
but all the luck was bad.
It left me bruised and beaten and
extremely sore and sad.

I knew I had to dump that penny
one way or another.
I'm feeling so much better since
I gave it to my brother.

Captain Impossible

Captain Impossible
likes to have fun
by learning to do things
that cannot be done.

He'll quack like a rabbit.
He'll bark like a cat.
He'll oink like a rooster
and moo like a rat.

He'll sniff with his fingers.
He'll taste with his toes.
He'll see with his elbows
and hear with his nose.

He'll draw a triangular,
circular square,
then sit on his shoulders
and stroll through the air.

He'll read with his eyes closed.
He'll run standing still.
He'll talk like a rock
as it rolls up a hill.

Impossible things...
he can do quite a few,
but *possible* things are
too boring to do.

And Captain Impossible
likes to have fun,
so, he won't read this poem
since *that* can be done.

My Mom Likes Playing DnD

My mom likes playing DnD
alone inside her room,
but doesn't have adventures
in a dungeon or a tomb.

She doesn't get together with
her friends to go on quests.
She doesn't battle monsters
and explore for treasure chests.

She doesn't conjure magic spells
like lightning balls and ice.
I'm pretty sure she doesn't even
own a set of dice.

And I don't think she's playing
as a halfling or an elf.
But still, she plays it every day,
and always by herself.

I think she might be playing
a completely different game.
The only thing it seems to have
in common is the name.

She'll shout, "I'm playing DnD.
This game is just superb,"
then hang a sign outside her door.
It reads, "Do Not Disturb."

My Mother Said to Clean My Room

My mother said to clean my room,
and so, I went and found the broom.
I also got a cleaning rag,
and for my trash, a garbage bag.

Then, next, I went and grabbed the mop
and filled a bucket to the top.
I got a scrubber and a sponge
to wipe the grime and scrub the grunge.

I found some soap and cleaning spray
to wipe the dirt and dust away,
some window cleaner for the glass
and polish made for shining brass.

I plugged the vacuum cleaner in.
I got a liner for the bin,
a roll of paper towels too,
and for my carpet, rug shampoo.

But gathering the things required
to clean my room has left me tired.
And so, I went to mom to say,
"I'll clean my room some other day."

Our Cat Likes the Vacuum

Our cat likes the vacuum.
He thinks that it's fun
to hop on and ride when
it's starting to run.

He'll go for a drive
as it's cleaning the ground
and purr as it circles
around and around.

It's like an amusement
park ride for a cat,
that chases our dog
and our little pet rat.

It makes him so happy.
It brings him such joy.
The vacuum is clearly
his favorite toy.

Then, last week, he learned how
to start the machine.
He rides it all day now.
Our floors are SO clean.

Helping the Teacher

Today we helped the teacher
with the things she has to do.
We graded all our homework
and erased the whiteboard too.

To clean and organize her desk,
we emptied every drawer.
We moved our chairs out to the hall
to sweep the classroom floor.

We think we might have accidentally
thrown her lunch away,
but it was looking old so that
was probably okay.

While stacking up her books so we
could dust the classroom shelves,
we spilled a box of glue and paint
and glitter on ourselves.

When she returned and saw our help
a tear rolled down her cheek.
She must have been so happy that
she couldn't even speak.

Online Is Fine

The schools are in session
but right now, at mine,
the teachers and students
are meeting online.

It's quite a bit different,
but I think it's cool,
since this way I'll never
be tardy to school.

My mom doesn't yell at me,
making a fuss,
that, if I don't hurry,
I might miss the bus.

To meet with my teacher
or talk to my tutor,
I roll out of bed and
turn on the computer.

I don't need my backpack,
my shoes, or my coat.
It saves so much time when
your school is remote.

I don't pack a lunch
and I don't take a shower,
which means I can sleep in
a whole extra hour.

Underneath an Apple Tree

Underneath an apple tree
one lovely day in autumn
a friend walked up to talk with me,
and then an apple got him.

It dropped and bonked him on the head,
which would have made me bawl.
But he just laughed and winked and said,
"That apple likes the fall."

Rules for School

Get to school before the bell.
In the classroom, do not yell.
In the hallway, do not run.
Make sure that your homework's done.

Tie your shoes and comb your hair.
Don't start dancing on your chair.
Don't draw pictures on the wall.
Don't ride skateboards in the hall.

Don't chew bubblegum in class.
Don't bring bugs in from the grass.
Don't say things you know are rude.
Never, ever throw your food.

These are rules you should obey.
As for me, I'm sad to say
that's a list of every rule
I forgot today at school.

Our Teacher's a Ghost

We have a new teacher.
We think she's a ghost.
Of all of the teachers,
she scares us the most.

The dress that she wears
looks a lot like a sheet.
It brushes the ground.
Does she even have feet?

She moans and she groans
at the students all day.
She boos if our schoolwork
is done the wrong way.

It's clear she's a ghost.
Though we weren't sure before,
we knew it the minute
she walked through the door.

I'm a Pirate and a Pumpkin

I'm a pirate and a pumpkin.
I'm a fairy and a frog.
I'm a robot and a skeleton,
a dragon and a dog.

I'm a mummy and a werewolf.
I'm a superhero too.
I'm a combination zombie
ballerina kangaroo.

I'm an alien, an astronaut,
a cowboy, and a queen.
Yes, I'm wearing all my costumes.
Man, it's cold this Halloween!

I'm Glad at Last It's Halloween

I'm glad at last it's Halloween.
Tonight will be a spooky scene
as ghosts and goblins roam the streets
in search of houses serving sweets.

I'll see some zombies dressed in rags
and mummies lugging candy bags,
a vampire here, a werewolf there,
a cyclops with a one-eyed stare.

Okay, I think I've changed my mind.
With all the monsters I might find,
I'd better stay in here and hide.
I'm much too scared to go outside.

I Dressed up as a Dinosaur

I dressed up as a dinosaur
for Halloween this year.
I thought I'd frighten everyone
and make them quake with fear.

I stomped and tromped around the house.
I raised my head and roared.
But no one seemed to notice me.
In fact, they all looked bored.

My father yawned and rolled his eyes.
My mother said, "That's cute."
My sister said, "Adorable!
I love your dino suit."

I thought they'd all be terrified
but they weren't scared at all
since no one minds a dinosaur
that's only three feet tall.

Thanksgiving Leftovers

We've got lots of food left
from Thanksgiving Day
from dozens of dishes
that filled our buffet.

There's...

Leftover turkey
and leftover ham,
leftover cranberries,
leftover lamb,
leftover salads
and scalloped potatoes,
leftover turnips
and trout and tomatoes,
cornbread and brown bread
and roast beef and peas,
baked beans and green beans
and one piece of cheese.

We've got lots of food left
but please tell me why...
Oh, why don't we have any
leftover pie?

The Sport for Me

I think I'd like to learn to ski.
It looks like just the sport for me.
I want the fun and all the thrills
of racing down those snowy hills.

I dream that, someday, I will see
those snowy hills and learn to ski.
But not today. That's how it goes
when, where you live, it never snows.

Snow Mail

My cousin's my pen pal.
We write back and forth.
My home's in the south and
she lives way up north.
The winter is windy
and white in her town.
All season it's freezing,
with snow swirling down.

She says when her city
is coated in snow,
the nights are enchanting,
with lights all aglow.
The snow sounds delightful!
I wish I could see.
I asked her if maybe
she'd send some to me.

She told me she boxed up
some snowballs and hail,
and shipped me the package
last week in the mail.
I'm wondering now...
did my cousin forget?
Her package arrived but was empty.
And wet.

With Christmas Coming Soon

With Christmas coming soon, I fear
I wasn't very good this year.
I didn't keep my bedroom clean.
I broke my brother's tambourine.
I stuck my sister with a pin.
I never turned my homework in.
At school, I scribbled on the walls
and rode my skateboard in the halls.

I yelled and ran around our house.
I scared my mother with a mouse.
I whined when she said, "Take a bath."
I didn't memorize my math.
I never listened to my dad.
I guess that I've been pretty bad.
And so, my parents both insist
that I'm on Santa's "Naughty List."

There's not much time, but I believe
I might be able, Christmas Eve,
to maybe muster up the power
to not be bad for half an hour.
Do you suppose that's long enough
to make up for the naughty stuff?
If not, I'll have another goal;
to find a way to sell some coal.

I Can't Believe It's Christmas Eve

I can't believe it's Christmas Eve
and everyone's awake
because, today, I'm sad to say,
we made a big mistake.

We went to bed but then, instead
of slumbering and dreaming,
we woke in fear, surprised to hear
the sound of Santa screaming.

And what a scare to see him there!
His Santa suit was smoking.
His Christmas sack and hat were black.
He coughed like he was choking.

He hit the ground and rolled around
until the fire was out,
then looked at us in mild disgust
and gave a little pout.

We felt so sad to see him mad.
It seems we were to blame.
And Santa Claus was mad because
his suit went up in flame.

The lesson here is pretty clear
and all of us are learning,
on Christmas Eve you shouldn't leave
the Christmas Yule log burning.

Santa's Feeling Sick

Daddy called the doctor,
and told him, "Please come quick.
Santa's in the living room
and feeling somewhat sick.

"Santa's slightly out of sorts.
He's looking rather ill,
showing certain symptoms
like a fever and a chill.

"Sad to say, he's shivering
as if he has the flu.
Please come look. I'm sure you'll know
exactly what to do."

Twenty minutes later,
when the doctor bustled in,
Santa got examined
from his elbow to his chin.

"Santa," said the doctor,
"It's as clear as it can be...
You've got tinselitis;
You're allergic to their tree."

A Fishy List

Christmas day, beneath our tree,
here's a list of what I see:

Feathers, tuna, toys with bells,
tasty treats with fishy smells,
scratching post and fluffy bed,
ball of yarn and spool of thread,
laser pointer, catnip, mouse,
comfy, cozy kitty house.

I hope next year I'll do better.
I wrote Santa Claus a letter
which he somehow must have missed.
Instead, he read my kitten's list.

My Brother Punched Me in the Head

My brother punched me in the head.
I hit him on the chin.
He whacked me on the back and so,
I kicked him in the shin.

I jabbed him in the abdomen.
He bopped me on the nose.
I socked him in the stomach and
he tromped on all my toes.

He hit me in the ribcage and
I slugged him in the gut.
He struck me on the shoulder so,
I kicked his you-know-what.

Our mother yelled at us to stop.
Our father looked upset.
We only do this once a year
but somehow, they forget.

They really ought to know by now
that this is just the way
my brother and I celebrate
each year on Boxing Day.

New Year's Promises

My promises this New Year's Day?

☑ To do my work before I play

☑ To brush my teeth

☑ To make my bed

☑ To comb the hair upon my head

☑ To try to keep my bedroom clean

☑ To be polite and never mean

And one more where I'm not so great...

☐ To put the right year in the date

January 1, _____

I'm Glad to Be Me

I'm glad to be me. Yes, I'm glad to be me.
There's nothing and no one that I'd rather be.
I'm glad I'm the person who knows what I know.
I'm glad that I'll go all the places I'll go.

I'm glad that I have all the thoughts that I think,
the foods that I eat, and the drinks that I drink.
I'm glad that I have all the friends that I've met,
the things that I've got, and the things that I'll get.

I'm glad to be someone who sees what I see.
I'm glad to be me. Yes, I'm glad to be me.
And one other thing that I'm glad about too...
I think that you're great and I'm glad that you're you.

Index

ABOUT THE AUTHOR

Children's Poet Laureate (2013-2015) Kenn
Nesbitt is the author of many books for children,
including *The Armpit of Doom, More Bears!, The
Tighty-Whitey Spider,* and *One Minute Till
Bedtime.* He is also the creator of the world's
most popular children's poetry website,
www.poetry4kids.com.

More Books by Kenn Nesbitt

One Minute till Bedtime – It's time for tuck-in, and your little one wants just one more moment with you—so fill it with something that will feed the imagination and send them off to sleep in a snap! Little Brown Books for Young Readers. ISBN: 978-0316341219.

Bigfoot Is Missing – Children's Poets Laureate J. Patrick Lewis and Kenn Nesbitt team up to offer a smart, stealthy tour of the creatures of shadowy myth and fearsome legend. Bigfoot, the Mongolian Death Worm, and the Loch Ness Monster number among the many creatures lurking within these pages. Chronicle Books. ISBN: 978-1452118956.

The Elephant Repairman – Seventy hilarious poems about magical toilets, tyrannosaurus teachers, supersonic sloths, pranks to play on parents, and much, much more. ISBN: 979-8843960919.

My Dog Likes to Disco – Seventy more hilarious poems about disco-dancing dogs, invisible kids, misbehaving phones, preposterous people, and much, much more. ISBN: 979-8714869594.

My Cat Knows Karate – Another seventy poems about goofy gadgets, kooky characters, funny families, insane situations, and much, much more. ISBN: 978-1720779346.

The Biggest Burp Ever – Seventy more poems about wacky animals, comical characters, funny families, silly situations, and much, much more. ISBN: 978-1500802011.

The Armpit of Doom – Seventy new poems about crazy characters, funny families, peculiar pets, comical creatures, and much, much more. ISBN: 978-1477590287.

MORE BEARS! – Kenn Nesbitt's picture book debut will have you laughing while shouting "More Bears!" along with the story's disruptive audience. Sourcebooks Jabberwocky. ISBN: 978-1402238352.

The Tighty-Whitey Spider: And More Wacky Animals Poems I Totally Made Up – With poems like and "I Bought Our Cat a Jetpack" and "My Dog Plays Invisible Frisbee," this collection shines with rhymes that are full of jokes, thrills, and surprises. Sourcebooks Jabberwocky. ISBN: 978-1402238338.

My Hippo Has the Hiccups: And Other Poems I Totally Made Up *My Hippo Has the Hiccups* contains over one hundred of Kenn's newest and best-loved poems. The dynamic CD brings the poems to life with Kenn reading his own poetry, cracking a joke or two, and even telling stories about how the poems came to be. Sourcebooks Jabberwocky. ISBN: 978-1402218095.

Revenge of the Lunch Ladies: The Hilarious Book of School Poetry – From principals skipping school to lunch ladies getting back at kids who complain about cafeteria food, school has never been so funny. Meadowbrook Press. ISBN: 978-1416943648.

When the Teacher Isn't Looking: And Other Funny School Poems *When the Teacher Isn't Looking* may be the funniest collection of poems about school ever written. This collection of poems by Kenn Nesbitt is sure to have you in stitches from start to finish. Meadowbrook Press. ISBN: 978-0684031286.

The Aliens Have Landed at Our School! – No matter what planet you live on, this book is packed with far-out, funny, clever poems guaranteed to give you a galactic case of the giggles. Meadowbrook Press. ISBN: 978-0689048647.

Made in the USA
Monee, IL
22 October 2024

7ba9685f-772c-4cb2-a9ac-46827e4b62a7R01